Busy
BOATS

To Ann-Janine, Caroline, and Suzanne—with thanks from Tony.
For Mister Mush and Scampy—A. P.

The Publisher thanks the National Maritime Museum, Greenwich, England, for
their kind assistance in the development of this book.

KINGFISHER
a Houghton Mifflin Company imprint
222 Berkeley Street
Boston, Massachusetts 02116
www.houghtonmifflinbooks.com

First published in hardcover in 2002
First published in paperback in 2005

10 9 8 7 6 5 4 3 2

Text copyright © Tony Mitton 2002
Illustrations copyright © Ant Parker 2002

LIBRARY OF CONGRESS CATALOGING-IN-PUBLICATION DATA
has been applied for.

ISBN 978-07534-5916-4

Printed in Taiwan

2TR/0307/SHENS/CG/158MA/C

Busy
BOATS

Tony Mitton and
Ant Parker

KINGFISHER

BOSTON

Boats are really wonderful for sailing us around.
They travel through the water
with a sloppy-slappy sound.

It's fun to go out boating, especially in the sun.
The water's cool and sparkly,
so come on, everyone!

A boat sits on the water
like an empty bowl or cup.
It's hollow and it's full of air,
and that's what keeps it up.

An anchor holds you steady
when you're bobbing in a bay.
You wind a chain to raise it
when you want to sail away.

Over lakes and seas and rivers,
wind blows very strong.
Some boats have sails to catch it
so it pushes them along.

To handle boats with masts and sails,
you need a clever crew.
The captain is the one in charge,
who tells them what to do.

A dinghy or a rowboat
is useful near the shore.

You make it travel backward
by pulling on each oar.

Whoosh!

A motorboat is powered
by propeller from the back.
It whooshes through the water
and leaves a foamy track.

And just in case, by accident,
you tumble from the boat,
you have to wear a life jacket,
made to help you float.

Some boats are built for fishing
where the ocean waves are steep.

Their nets are cast to catch the fish,
then haul them from the deep.

A ship can carry cargo,
which is loaded at the docks.

Heave ho! Look out below!
Here comes a giant box.

A ferry carries cars and trucks
to where they need to go.

The people travel up above.
The vehicles stay below.

A mighty ocean liner
has a big and busy crew.
It carries many passengers.
They're waving now. Yoo-hoo!

The ship has cozy cabins
where the passengers can stay.
And out on deck they stroll around
and watch the sea or play.

But when the journey's over—
Ahoy! The lighthouse rock!

The ship glides into harbor
and ties up at the dock.

Boat parts

lighthouse

this is a tall building on the coast with a flashing light to guide ships and keep them away from rocks

anchor

this is a very heavy piec of metal with hooks that dig into the ground unde the water and stop the boat from drifting away

propeller

this has **blades** that spin around very fast at the back of the boat and push against the water to move the boat forward

oars

these are long poles with flat **blade** on the end that push against the water to move the boat forward

deck

this is the floor of a boat

cabin

this is the little room where you sleep on board a boat

cargo

this is the name fo the goods that a ship carries

MANDY

name

many boats are given names by their owners